D1071081

Capstone
7/30/09

CONQUERING ENGLAND
THE BATTLE OF HASTINGS

BY BARBARA DAVIS

CONSULTANT:
Steven Isaac
Associate Professor of Medieval History
Longwood University
Farmville, Virginia

Capstone
press®
Mankato, Minnesota

Edge Books are published by Capstone Press,
151 Good Counsel Drive, P.O. Box 669, Mankato, Minnesota 56002.
www.capstonepress.com

Library of Congress Cataloging-in-Publication Data
Davis, Barbara J., 1952–
    Conquering England: the Battle of Hastings/by Barbara Davis.
    p. cm. — (Bloodiest battles.)
    Includes bibliographical references and index.
    Summary: "Describes events before, during, and after the Battle of Hastings,
including key players, weapons, and battle tactics." — Provided by publisher.
    ISBN-13: 978-1-4296-1940-0 (hardcover)
    ISBN-10: 1-4296-1940-6 (hardcover)
    1. Hastings, Battle of, England, 1066 — Juvenile literature. I. Title. II. Title:
Battle of Hastings. III. Series.
DA196.D38 2009
942.02'1 — dc22   2008000527

Editorial Credits
Mandy Robbins, editor; Bob Lentz, designer/illustrator; Kim Brown,
    production designer; Jo Miller, photo researcher

Photo Credits
Alamy/David Chedgy, 11; Manor Photography/Robert Slade, 28; Mary Evans
    Picture Library, 7, 15, 16, 26
Art Resource, N.Y./Erich Lessing, 24–25
Corbis/Bettmann, 8
Corbis/Historical Picture Archive, 4
Getty Images Inc./Hulton Archive, 18, 23
Mary Evans Picture Library, cover (both)

1 2 3 4 5 6 13 12 11 10 09 08

TABLE OF CONTENTS

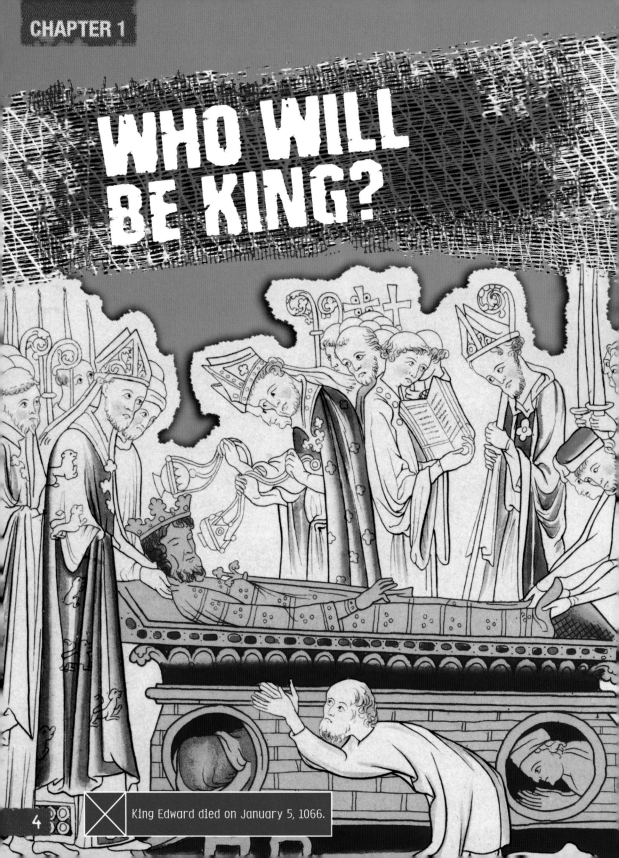

CHAPTER 1

WHO WILL BE KING?

King Edward died on January 5, 1066.

On a cold January day in 1066, King Edward of England lay dying. The king had no son to replace him. Three powerful men wanted to be the next king of England. One was Harold Godwinsson. One was Duke William of Normandy. The last was Harald Hardrada of Norway. All three were famous warriors. All three were willing to wage bloody war to get what they wanted.

A Local Leader

Harold Godwinsson was an **Anglo-Saxon**. He was one of the wealthiest men in England. He was also trusted and well-liked by the people. The Anglo-Saxons wanted Harold Godwinsson to be England's next king. The people got their wish the day after King Edward's death, when Harold was crowned the new king of England.

Anglo-Saxon — a member of a group of people with German ancestry who once occupied England

The Duke

In northern France, Duke William of Normandy was furious when he heard that Godwinsson had been crowned king. Duke William claimed that King Edward had promised the throne to him years earlier. William decided to bring his **Norman** warriors to England and take the crown by force.

A Viking Warrior

In Norway, Harald Hardrada swore to win the English crown. He was the king of Norway and a fierce Viking warrior. Hardrada claimed that a previous English king had promised the throne to Hardrada's **predecessor**. Because of this, Hardrada believed that he had the right to be king of England.

Norman — a member of a group of people with Scandinavian ancestry who lived in northern France

predecessor — the man who had served as the king of Norway before Hardrada

Duke William of Normandy inherited his title at the age of 7.

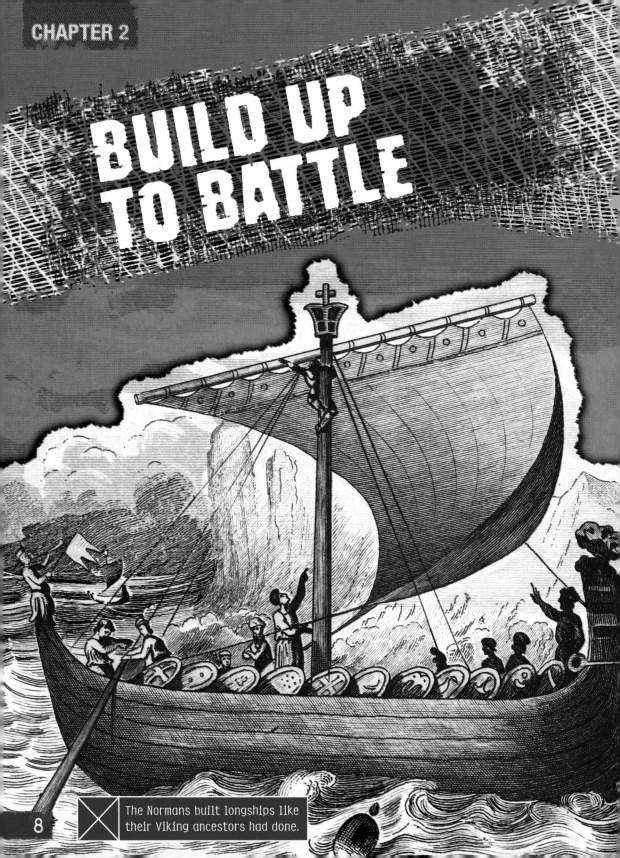

CHAPTER 2

BUILD UP TO BATTLE

The Normans built longships like their Viking ancestors had done.

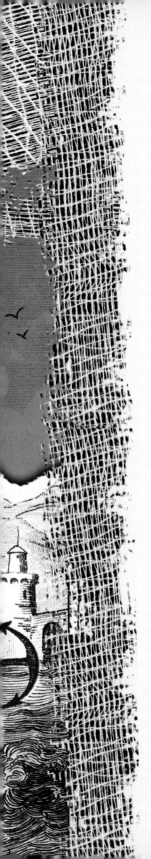

Duke William quickly began planning his invasion of England. He commanded all of his knights to bring fighting men and supplies. A knight was a professional warrior who owed his king military service. The knight's job was to fight for and protect the king. William also hired **mercenaries** for the battle. He promised wealth and land in England to everyone who would fight with him.

William commanded shipbuilders to build a fleet of warships. These ships would transport his army across the English Channel. The shipbuilders began their work at the mouth of the Dives River in Normandy. Soon, hundreds of ships floated in the water.

mercenary — a warrior who is hired and paid for military service

Waiting on the Wind

William's fleet of ships faced England. His soldiers were ready to attack. But they had to postpone their plans. The wind was blowing in the wrong direction to allow passage to England.

Finally, after weeks of waiting, the breeze shifted. Sails swelled with air. Knights, servants, and horses scrambled to get on the ships. Smaller boats, loaded with supplies, squeezed between the bigger warships.

On September 27, 1066, William's fleet left the harbor. The ships carried more than 2,000 horses and about 10,000 soldiers, as well as many servants.

Godwinsson Prepares for Battle

Godwinsson knew a battle was coming, and he had been preparing as well. Like William, he had men who owed him military service. This group was called the *fyrd*. Godwinsson also had **huscarls** to protect him.

huscarl — a professional soldier who served as a personal bodyguard to Scandinavian and Anglo-Saxon nobles

Norman knights and Anglo-Saxon
huscarls wore armor and helmets.

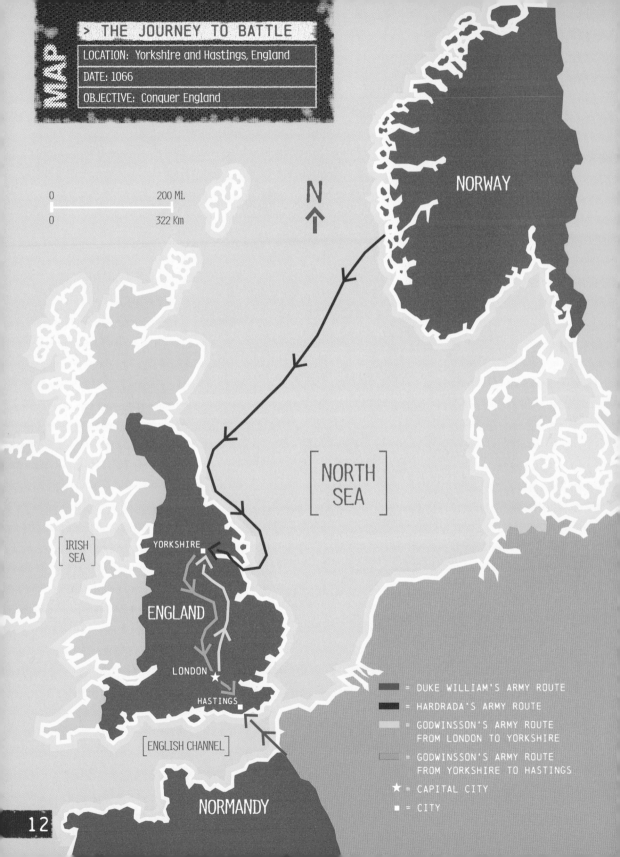

> THE JOURNEY TO BATTLE

LOCATION: Yorkshire and Hastings, England

DATE: 1066

OBJECTIVE: Conquer England

0 ——— 200 Mi.

0 ——— 322 Km

N

NORWAY

NORTH SEA

IRISH SEA

YORKSHIRE

ENGLAND

LONDON

HASTINGS

[ENGLISH CHANNEL]

NORMANDY

■ = DUKE WILLIAM'S ARMY ROUTE

■ = HARDRADA'S ARMY ROUTE

■ = GODWINSSON'S ARMY ROUTE FROM LONDON TO YORKSHIRE

■ = GODWINSSON'S ARMY ROUTE FROM YORKSHIRE TO HASTINGS

★ = CAPITAL CITY

■ = CITY

Vikings Attack!

While Godwinsson focused on the upcoming battle with Duke William, Hardrada made his move. He landed in northern England with 7,000 Vikings. Hardrada and his men surprised the Anglo-Saxon soldiers guarding Yorkshire.

The screaming Vikings attacked the Anglo-Saxons. The Anglo-Saxons fought bravely, but eventually, the Vikings claimed victory.

Race to the North

Upon learning of the attack on Yorkshire, Godwinsson led his army north. They marched 200 miles (322 kilometers) in four days. Godwinsson's forces surprised the Vikings at Stamford Bridge, near Yorkshire.

The Vikings had been celebrating their victory for days. They barely had time to grab their weapons before the Anglo-Saxons attacked. Although the Vikings fought hard, the Anglo-Saxons chased them back across the bridge. During the battle, Hardrada was killed. The now leaderless Vikings retreated to their ships and left England.

FACT:

> HARALD HARDRADA

Harald Hardrada was as fierce a ruler as he was a warrior. His real name was Harald Sigurdsson, but people called him *Hardrada*, which means "hard ruler."

Another Enemy Arrives

On September 28, 1066, Duke William and his army sailed into Pevensey Harbor in England. The Normans expected to see Godwinsson and his army ready for battle. **Archers** jumped into the shallow water along the beach. They were ready to protect the knights and foot soldiers getting off the ships.

To William's surprise, there was no enemy army to meet them. Godwinsson and his forces were still in northern England. After a few days, William moved his army north along the coast, attacking and destroying villages. He hoped Godwinsson would rush back to defend his people before rebuilding a strong army.

Race to the South

When news of the Normans' arrival reached Godwinsson, he led his army to meet the Norman threat. Many Anglo-Saxon soldiers had been killed or injured fighting the Vikings. Godwinsson needed replacements. He sent messengers to all of the towns and villages along the route south. Soon, more soldiers joined the Anglo-Saxon forces.

archer — a soldier trained to shoot arrows from a bow

When the Normans arrived in England, they expected Anglo-Saxon warriors to meet them.

15

Duke William of Normandy and his knights fought on horseback.

Godwinsson's Strategy

Godwinsson waited for the Normans on top of Senlac Hill, 6 miles (10 kilometers) north of Hastings. This position would force the Normans to fight uphill.

Godwinsson had about 7,000 men. These warriors fought on foot using swords, battle-axes, and lances. They formed lines several rows deep across the ridge. The most experienced fighters were in the front. The rest of the army waited behind them. Godwinsson was ready to fight right alongside his men.

Duke William's Strategy

Duke William split his army into three sections. In each section, the archers stood in front. Foot soldiers were in the middle. Knights were in the back.

Unlike the Anglo-Saxons, Norman knights fought on horseback. Their horses were trained for battle. Knights could quickly get close to the enemy and then speed away. William was depending on his mounted knights to help win the battle.

FACT:

> **WARHORSES**

Warhorses could carry between 300 and 400 pounds (136 and 181 kilograms). This was the weight of a fully-armored knight and his weapons.

CHAPTER 3

BATTLE TO THE DEATH

During the battle at Senlac Hill, the Norman knights slammed into the Anglo-Saxon shield wall again and again.

LEARN ABOUT

> BATTLE FEVER
> THE SHIELD WALL
> A GREAT LEADER FALLS

Finally, both sides met at Senlac Hill. The Normans looked up at their opponents from the bottom of the ridge. The Anglo-Saxons glared down from the top.

At Godwinsson's command, the front row of Anglo-Saxon warriors brought up their shields. The edges of the shields overlapped. The result was a long wall of strong shields. The eager Anglo-Saxons began hitting their weapons against their shields. The Normans added the blare of brass horns to the noise. Anglo-Saxon warriors roared insults at the Norman forces. Normans shouted insults back. Warhorses stomped at the ground and whinnied. Battle fever had taken hold.

Suddenly, Norman arrows whistled toward the Anglo-Saxons. The battle had begun.

Up Against the Shield Wall

William thought the storm of arrows would injure many of the Anglo-Saxons. But the Norman archers were firing uphill and from too far away. Most of their arrows thudded into the strong Anglo-Saxon shields. William ordered the foot soldiers to advance.

The Norman foot soldiers ran toward the Anglo-Saxons. Once the Normans got close, the Anglo-Saxons threw rocks, battle-axes, and spears at them. The Normans threw themselves against the Anglo-Saxon shields. They thrust their swords into any openings they could find in the shield wall. The Anglo-Saxons swung their weapons with deadly force. Their battle-axes easily sliced through Norman helmets and armor.

> **FACT:**

> **ANGLO-SAXON BATTLE-AX**

The wood handle of the Anglo-Saxon battle-ax was usually 2 to 3 feet (0.6 to 1 meter) long. Swinging this long handle, a strong fighter could crack a human skull through an iron helmet.

MARSHY AREA

0   300 YD.

0   274 M.

N

SENLAC HILL

ROAD TO LONDON

TELHAM HILL

= ANGLO-SAXON ARMY

= NORMAN ARMY

= ROAD

Thundering Hooves

William's foot soldiers could not break through the shield wall. He sent his mounted knights to charge against the Anglo-Saxon line.

Most Anglo-Saxon warriors had little experience with warhorses. The sight of these huge beasts charging at them was terrifying. The ground shook from the horses' pounding hooves. Still, the brave Anglo-Saxons held the shield wall together.

One Final Push

As the day went on, the armies continued fighting. The Anglo-Saxons held their line. The Normans were getting tired. William rallied all of his fighters for one final push. If this advance failed, William knew the Anglo-Saxons would claim victory.

William sent his archers up the hill to collect the arrows they had fired at the beginning of the battle. Once again, the archers fired their arrows. This time, though, they were closer to the Anglo-Saxons.

> RUMORS SPREAD

At one point in the battle, a rumor spread through the Norman forces that William had been killed. To rally his troops, William rode through the ranks with his helmet off to prove he was alive.

FACT

The Normans' arrows fell like deadly rain onto the Anglo-Saxons. One arrow struck Godwinsson above his eye.

At one end of the shield wall, the Norman forces acted as though they were retreating. Believing the Normans were fleeing, some Anglo-Saxon warriors broke away from the shield wall. Yelling and swinging their battle-axes, they chased the Normans down the hill. This created a gap in the shield wall.

When Godwinsson was struck by a Norman arrow, it was a turning point in the battle.

The Normans took advantage of the opening in the shield wall.

Norman knights drove their horses through the Anglo-Saxon lines.

They wanted to kill Godwinsson.

According to some sources, Godwinsson died instantly from

his arrow wound. According to others, he was just wounded. The

huscarls then tried to protect Godwinsson from the Norman

knights. They fought bravely. But, one by one, the huscarls were killed.

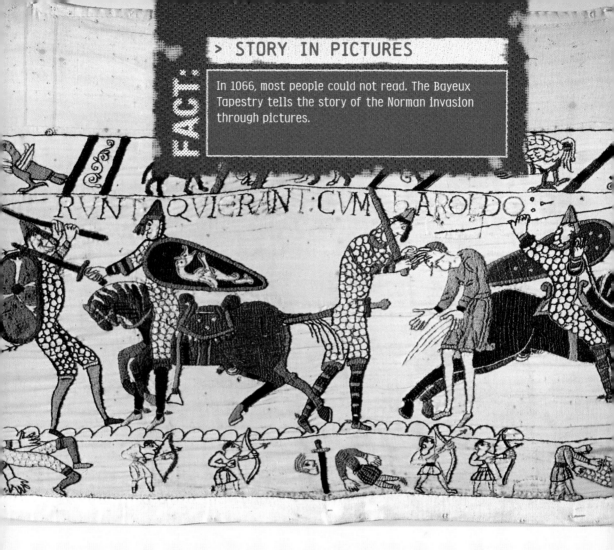

> STORY IN PICTURES

In 1066, most people could not read. The Bayeux Tapestry tells the story of the Norman invasion through pictures.

RVNT QVI ERANT CVM HAROLDO

When the Normans reached Godwinsson, they attacked. In minutes, the king lay dead. No one knows which account is true.

Godwinsson's death shook the spirit of the remaining Anglo-Saxons. Many of the nobles and the huscarls fell to the Normans. Soon, there was no one to command the *fyrd* soldiers. Not knowing what to do, the soldiers in the *fyrd* fled from the bloody battlefield.

CHAPTER 4

ENGLAND'S NEW KING

William was crowned king in Westminster Abbey, a religious building that King Edward had ordered to be built.

Life changed forever for the Anglo-Saxon people after the Battle of Hastings. William was crowned King of England on December 25, 1066. He wasted no time forcing his will on the Anglo-Saxons. Many Anglo-Saxon nobles had died in the battle of Hastings. William gave their land to Norman knights.

The Anglo-Saxons faced challenges to their language and customs as well. The Anglo-Saxons spoke English, but the Normans spoke French. As a result, French became the language spoken in government meetings and in churches.

Many people believe that the ruins
of Battle Abbey are haunted.

The Normans also brought a new system of government to England. Under this system, the king had more power than before. The new Norman nobles owed their land and possessions to the king. Because of this, King William expected loyalty and support for all of his decisions.

A few groups of Anglo-Saxons formed small armies of resistance and struck at the Normans whenever they could. William spent years crushing this resistance.

Yet William did have a certain respect for the Anglo-Saxon people. He ordered the building of Battle Abbey so people would remember the Battle of Hastings. He wanted to honor the worthy opponents his army had fought. William ordered the altar in the abbey to be built on the exact spot where Godwinsson had died.

FACT:

> **BATTLE ABBEY**

The first building of Battle Abbey completed was the church. It was finished in 1094, but King William did not live to see it.

GLOSSARY

Anglo-Saxon (ANG-glow SAKS-son) — a member of a group of people with German ancestry who once occupied England

archer (AHR-chur) — a person who shoots a bow and arrow

English Channel (ING-lish CHAN-uhl) — a narrow strip of the Atlantic Ocean that separates the British Isles from the rest of the continent of Europe

huscarl (HUSS-carl) — a professional soldier who served as a personal bodyguard to Scandinavian and Anglo-Saxon nobles

mercenary (MUR-suh-nayr-ee) — a soldier who is paid to fight for a foreign army

Norman (NOHR-man) — a member of a group of people with Scandinavian ancestry who moved to northern France in the 900s

predecessor (PRED-uh-sess-ur) — someone who held an office or a job before another person

READ MORE

Hilliam, Paul. *Medieval Weapons and Warfare: Armies and Combat in Medieval Times.* Library of the Middle Ages. New York: Rosen, 2004.

Macdonald, Fiona. *Warfare in the Middle Ages.* Battle Zones. Columbus, Ohio: Peter Bedrick Books, 2004.

Martin, Michael. *Knights.* Warriors of History. Mankato, Minn.: Capstone Press, 2007.

INTERNET SITES

FactHound offers a safe, fun way to find Internet sites related to this book. All of the sites on FactHound have been researched by our staff.

Here's how:

1. Visit *www.facthound.com*
2. Choose your grade level.
3. Type in this book ID **1429619406** for age-appropriate sites. You may also browse subjects by clicking on letters, or by clicking on pictures and words.
4. Click on the **Fetch It** button.

FactHound will fetch the best sites for you!

INDEX